Published by Creative Education
123 South Broad Street, Mankato, Minnesota 56001
Creative Education is an imprint of The Creative Company

Art direction by Rita Marshall
Production design by Clean Tone Creative Consultants

Photographs by: Allsport (Brian Bahr, Al Bello, Clive Brunskill,
Stu Forster, John Gichigi, Hulton Archive, Jed Jacobsohn, Ken Levine,
Gary M. Prior, Ezra Shaw, Jamie Squire, Matthew Stockman),
Getty Images (Al Bello, Phil Cole, Paul Harris/Online USA, Mike Hewitt,
Chris Hondros/Newsmakers, Ken Levine, Donald Miralle, Online USA,
Ezra Shaw, Stringer), Icon Sports Media (Gary I. Rothstein/WireImage.com,
Preston Mack).

Library of Congress Cataloging-in-Publication Data

Franzen, Lenore.
Venus Williams / by Lenore Franzen.
p. cm. – (Ovations)
Summary: Discusses the life and career of tennis star Venus Williams.
ISBN 1-58341-249-2

1. Williams, Venus, 1980-–Juvenile literature. 2. Tennis players–
United States–Biography–Juvenile literature. 3. African-American
women tennis players–Biography–Juvenile literature. [1. Williams,
Venus, 1980- 2. Tennis players. 3. African Americans–Biography.
4. Women–Biography.] I. Title. II. Series.

GV994.W49 F73   2003
796.342'0973–dc21   2002031490

First Edition

2   4   6   8   9   7   5   3   1

OVATIONS

VENUS

WILLIAMS

BY LENORE FRANZEN

Creative Education

WILLIAMS

REFLECTIONS

Her father once said that a champion must be rough, tough, strong, and mentally sound. Venus Williams has all of those qualities. She combines unshakeable confidence and exceptional ability with a healthy balance between tennis and life outside the game.

Some call her arrogant, but Venus has always believed she can be the best. Her parents instilled that belief in her when she first picked up a racket, and soon Venus set out to climb to the top of a predominantly white, rich-person's sport. Nothing would stop her, and nothing did.

The athleticism she displays on the court is the best that women's tennis has ever seen. At 6-foot-2 (188 cm), Venus is towering, fierce, graceful, and everywhere her opponents try to place

the ball. She developed her trademark power by practicing with male pros. Her serves have been described as leaving a "vapor trail," they fly by so fast, and her deep ground strokes often prevent others from storming the net.

Still, Venus's life contains more than tennis. Her father, who has also served as her coach, insisted on balance from the beginning. "I'm not going to let Venus pass up on her childhood," he said. "Long after tennis is over, I want her to know who she is."

So far, he has succeeded. Venus earns top grades in school and plans to be a fashion designer after retiring from the game. She enjoys learning different languages, loves to cook, surf, play guitar, and romp with her Yorkshire terrier. Now at the peak of her sport, Venus Williams is starting to look beyond the tennis court and see an even greater world waiting for her, one full of possibilities.

Venus plays to win, whether the prize is the U.S. Open trophy, opposite, or a kiss from her dog, Bob, above.

EVOLUTION

Nearly all top women tennis players are white. Most come from wealthy families, play at private clubs, and are pushed into the pros and a grueling tournament schedule. Venus never fit that mold.

Venus Ebone Starr Williams was born on June 17, 1980, the fourth of five daughters to Richard and Oracene Williams. Her family lived in Compton, California, a neighborhood marked by gangs, violence, and drugs. When she started playing tennis at age four, she used the free public courts, which were cracked and covered with graffiti. Out of these humble beginnings came a girl who would become the best in the sport.

Inspired by a woman tennis player he saw on TV, Richard Williams decided to teach his five daughters the game. The first three showed little

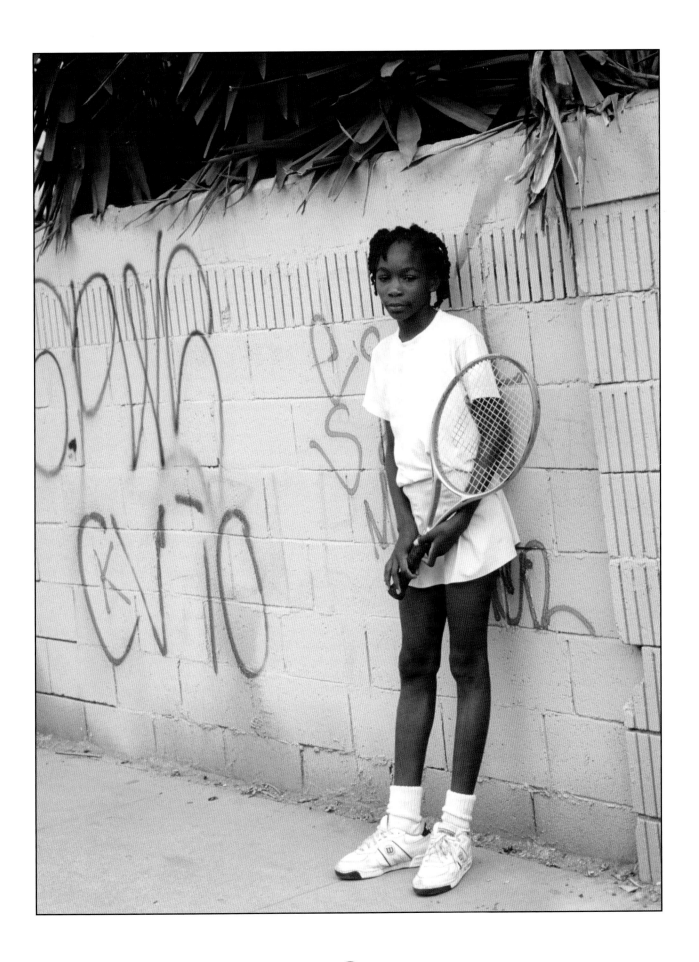

interest in swinging a racket, but the two younger sisters, Venus and Serena, took to the sport immediately. Venus hit every ball and then cried for more. She played so much that her father took her racket away from her a year later. "When someone loves something too much, it's more detrimental than a person who doesn't love it at all," he commented.

Richard and Oracene believed in strong family values. As a result, Venus and her sisters were raised in the Jehovah's Witness faith, which forbids drinking, smoking, gambling, or doing drugs. The couple also wanted their children to have a normal childhood. To keep Venus grounded in the "real world," they limited her practice time to two and a half hours, three times a week. Richard had seen too many other young girls burn out from tennis, and he didn't want Venus to lose her joy of playing. "Sure, I could have a superstar at 14," he said. "And I'm going to have nothing but a problem at 22."

By the time she was six, Venus thought she was going to be number 1. Every chance she could, Venus played with her younger sister, Serena. At first, they had to dodge bullets from fights that erupted nearby. But gradually the girls became a source of pride for the people of Compton. Gang members even guarded the courts while Venus and Serena practiced.

Venus laid the foundation for her game in her pre-teen years under the guidance of her father, Richard Williams, middle and opposite bottom.

Tall for her age and fast, Venus showed tremendous power. When she began playing in area junior tournaments, she proved unbeatable. Opponents struggled to return her serve. If they did, she was waiting at the net, ready to put the ball away. By the time she turned 10, she had already won the southern California girls' 12-and-under title. Clearly, she needed a bigger challenge.

THE EXPERIMENT

When Venus turned 11, her father decided she shouldn't play in any more junior tournaments. He believed that too much competitive tennis would interfere with his daughter's ability to learn and experiment on the court. He also worried that she would be distracted from her education and from pursuing other interests. No tennis player, male or female, had ever become a superstar without competing in the junior circuit. Could Venus develop her skills while playing in isolation, without the pressures tournaments provided?

In 1991, the family moved to Florida, where Venus could receive better training. The $2,200 monthly tuition to attend the International

Tennis Academy near Orlando was waived because of her exceptional ability. Her first coach (other than her father) was Rick Macci, who had scouted Venus in California. "I could see a Michael Jordan-type quality to her even then," he said.

The "experiment" continued, and the world of professional tennis watched. Venus kept up with her studies, usually maintaining A's in her classes. When she was 13, her parents home-schooled her to accommodate her busy practice schedule. She often played six hours a day, six days a week. For Venus, practice wasn't over until she'd hit 200 serves. Instead of travelling to tournaments, Venus began speaking to children at inner-city schools. "I know I should go back there," she said, "because that's where I'm from."

Venus turned pro at age 14. She had had no tournament experience for three years and was considered the best player nobody had ever heard of.

Her parents allowed her to turn pro on one condition: she maintain her A average in the private school where she was now enrolled. Her father also wanted to protect her from physical injury—common among young athletes who are pushed too hard—so he limited the number of events Venus could play in. Most pros her age averaged 14 tournaments a year; Venus played in four.

In the second round of her first professional tournament, Venus faced Arantxa Sanchez-Vicario, the world's number 2 player. Instead of being intimidated by the seasoned pro, Venus took the first set before losing the match. The tennis world was impressed with the newcomer's performance. Within a year, Venus was ranked 321 by the Women's Tennis Association.

In 1995, at the age of 15, Venus signed a $12 million endorsement deal with Reebok. She became a spokesmodel for the sporting goods company, wearing the newest tennis outfits—some she designed—and footwear.

That same year, little sister Serena turned pro, showing as much talent and determination as Venus. People took note of Serena's muscular

Off court, Venus and her sister Serena, above right, are each other's strongest supporters, but on the court, even Serena isn't safe from Venus's monster volleys.

build and powerful backhand and predicted that one day the sisters would face each other in a major tournament.

Except for competing in five tournaments in 1996, Venus stayed in Florida, went to high school, and practiced at the academy. Despite limited competition, Venus saw her rating jump from 321 to 207 in just one year.

THE WILLIAMS SHOW

Tennis has four major annual tournaments, called the Grand Slam events. They are the Australian Open, the French Open, Wimbledon, and the U.S. Open. In 1997, Venus competed in three of these tournaments and eliminated top players in early rounds. Each appearance boosted her standing. After the French Open in early June, Venus was ranked 90. After Wimbledon in July, she moved to 66.

At the U.S. Open, 17-year-old Venus made history on several fronts. First, she reached the finals for the first time as a pro. Second, she was the tournament's first unseeded player to make it to the finals. And third, she

was the first black woman to play in the championship match since Althea Gibson in 1958. Venus lost to Martina Hingis (0–6, 4–6), but her remarkable progress lifted her to number 27. She was closing in on her goal.

Off court, Venus continued her education. She graduated from high school and began taking courses at the area community college. She and Serena also started to write and publish a newsletter, *Tennis Monthly Recap*, for the professional players on tour and for interested subscribers.

As sisters and best friends, Venus and Serena shared everything, including their desire to be the best. Serena was posing an impressive, if less-disciplined, threat to Venus's position, narrowing the gap in their rankings with an aggressive, in-your-face style of play. Yet the sisters maintained a fierce loyalty to each other. "Family comes first," said Venus, "no matter how many times we play each other. Nothing will come between me and my sister."

In January 1998, at the Australian Open, Venus won her first important tennis title. She paired with American Justin Gimelstob to win the mixed doubles event. This tournament also proved notable because the Williamses, who faced off in a second-round singles match, were the first black sisters to compete against each other in a professional event.

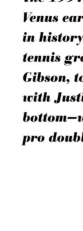

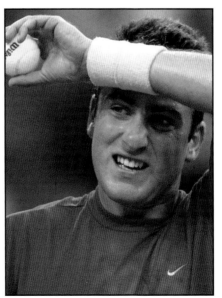

The 1997 season saw Venus earn a place in history alongside tennis great Althea Gibson, top, and—with Justin Gimelstob, bottom—win her first pro doubles title.

Venus won again two months later, scoring her first professional singles title, at the age of 17, in the IGA Tennis Classic against South African Joannette Kruger, 6–3, 6–2. In April, at the Lipton Championship, Venus clobbered 16-year-old Russian Anna Kournikova for her second singles title.

Tournament wins were paying off, pushing Venus's ranking up to number 5. Her serves were also shaking up the tennis world. In a match against Mary Pierce in Zurich, Switzerland, Venus hit an ace that was clocked at 127 miles (204 km) per hour, the fastest ever in women's tennis and faster than many men's serves.

In May 1998, Venus defeated Serena in their second meeting, this time in the quarterfinals of the Italian Open. Unfortunately, Venus went on to lose to top-ranked Hingis in what the press called "the hottest rivalry in women's tennis." Hingis acknowledged Venus's power and tenacity. "She didn't give up until the end."

Early in 1999, Venus and Serena found themselves in the finals of two separate tournaments on the same day, with a chance to make history if they won. Serena captured her first career singles victory at the Gaz de France, and, inspired by the news, Venus successfully defended her crown in the IGA Classic.

The Williams sisters dominated tennis tournaments around the world in the late 1990s with their power serves, deadly strokes, and unwavering confidence.

Then, a month later, Venus and Serena found themselves playing each other in the Lipton Championship. Their father was so proud of them that he waved a sign from the stands that read, "Welcome to the Williams Show." Venus prevailed 6–1, 4–6, 6–4.

In June, the Williams sisters went to the French Open, ready to avenge Venus's loss to Hingis in the quarterfinals the year before. They defeated Hingis and Kournikova for the doubles title. Their victory marked the first time sisters had won a Grand Slam doubles title in the history of tennis.

Fueled by this win, the sisters came to the U.S. Open armed for battle. After a three-set struggle, Venus succumbed to Hingis in the semifinals. But the Williamses had the last word. Serena advanced to the finals and overpowered Hingis in two sets. Together, the sisters also won the women's doubles title. Suddenly, Venus was ranked number 3, Serena, number 4.

Unfortunately, 15 years of playing had taken a physical toll on Venus. In November 1999, she was diagnosed with tendonitis in both wrists. At that point, on the advice of doctors, friends, and family, Venus decided to give her body a much-needed rest and took the next six months off.

Her absence didn't seem to hurt her game. In July 2000, she eliminated every opponent, including Serena, to reach the prestigious Wimbledon finals. There, on the grass courts in England, Venus defeated Lindsey Davenport 6–3, 7–6 for the singles title and her first Grand Slam victory. Again, she and Serena proved unbeatable in doubles.

"There's been so few black people to win Wimbledon or even just play outstanding tennis," said Venus. "We're going to do our best to change that."

At the U.S. Open two months later, Venus denied her sister the women's singles title Serena had captured the year before. Venus credited her time off as helping to intensify her game. "I'm a different competitor than I was in the past," she said. "I think it's just about an attitude, the kind of attitude you take out there toward your game, toward everything, and it paid off."

Then, at the 2000 Olympics in Sydney, Australia, Venus took the gold in singles, and the sisters earned gold medals in the women's doubles. For the next several months, Venus went on a 32-match winning streak.

Reebok recognized Venus's exceptional ability and signed the 20-year-old to another contract, this time worth $40 million—the richest deal ever for a female athlete.

Venus had plenty to smile about in 2000: renewed physical and emotional strength, twin titles at Wimbledon, twin gold Olympic medals, and a huge endorsement deal.

In March 2001, controversy struck the Williams family. Four minutes before the start of the Evert Cup semifinal match in Indian Wells, California, Venus withdrew from playing Serena, claiming a knee injury, which her trainer later confirmed. Serena advanced to the finals. But then, the mood in the stands turned ugly. Whenever Serena won a point, the crowd of 16,000 booed. Nevertheless, Serena won the women's singles title. Some people accused Richard Williams of "fixing" the outcome of the match, though nothing was ever proven. Racial threats and insults reportedly circulated during play.

The story of the Williamses had always been tinged with controversy. Venus and Serena were black in a mostly white sport. Richard Williams closely managed his daughters' careers and often openly challenged the tennis establishment. The sisters' confidence and aloofness put some players off. But fortunately, these issues usually took a backseat to the Williamses' phenomenal ability on the court.

After the Evert Cup, Richard Williams decided that, whenever possible, Venus and Serena should play in

different tournaments to avoid having to face each other in key matches. Venus tried not to let these controversies distract her from her game, but she suffered early-round losses in the French Open and the Australian Open. By July, she had recovered, ousting eighth-seeded Justine Henin of Belgium 6–2, 3–6, 6–0 to claim her second Wimbledon singles title. All who watched the match said that Venus, now 21, may have played her best tennis ever that day. Her ranking held at number 2.

Given how well both sisters were playing, they were destined to face each other in a Grand Slam final. Sure enough, Venus and Serena met in the 2001 U.S. Open finals, where Venus dominated for the second straight year. At the end of the match, former black tennis champion Althea Gibson offered her assessment: "I would like to congratulate the Williamses for accomplishing this historic achievement. Two family members and two sisters who have become two of the greatest tennis athletes in the world." The televised center court match also signaled the first time a major network had aired the women's final, not the men's, in prime time.

Venus started out slow in 2002. At the Australian Open, she lost in the quarterfinals to Monica Seles. She recovered quickly, however, and

reached the finals of the French Open. Venus was defeated by sister Serena, but she finally accumulated enough tournament points to earn the long-desired number 1 ranking, becoming the first black player to do so since Arthur Ashe in 1975.

Not surprisingly, Venus and Serena were the top-seeded players at Wimbledon a few weeks later and reached the finals. In one of their best matchups, Serena again dominated, winning 7–6, 6–3, and claimed the number 1 world ranking. Venus paired with her sister to win the doubles title.

As the defending champion, Venus went into the 2002 U.S. Open hoping to earn her third consecutive title. She advanced to the finals, where again she faced her sister. With better first serves and fewer errors, Serena defeated Venus 6–4, 6–3.

When asked how it felt to lose to her younger sister, Venus smiled graciously and said, "I'm really happy for her." Eight years as a professional player had taught her that there is more to tennis than winning and more to life than tennis.

Venus Williams has established so many firsts in the game that women's tennis will never be the same. Out of a tough, inner-city start, she spun a fortune in earnings and endorsements. In a traditionally white sport, she has rewritten many of the rules that once determined whether a player succeeded. Venus has brought unmatched power and athleticism to tennis, raising the bar for other players for years to come. And she has done so with determination, grace, and complete confidence. Her legacy to the sport may well be that she brought down many barriers for African-American players.

When she isn't focused on tennis, Venus thinks of the future. She has considered retiring by age 26 so she can pursue other interests. Already she has designed her own line of clothes for Wilson Leather. With her lucrative earnings she has supported a tennis academy in south-central Los Angeles and other educational programs in North Carolina and Texas. Venus has proved to the world that whatever she sets her mind to, she will accomplish.

Now at the top of her sport, the determined woman from Compton is investing in the future of tennis by sharing her time and money with disadvantaged youth.

VOICES

ON PLAYING THE GAME:

"I like the way it makes you think.
And I like to blast the ball."
Venus Williams

"She's the runaway pick as our Female
Player of the Year, not merely because
of her 41–4 record, but because in
2000, she discovered an inner resolve,
as powerful as her monstrous forehand
swing volley."
Rachel Alexander,
Tennis *writer*

ON ATTITUDE:

"She has the strength, confidence, and
arrogance you need to become the top
player in the world."
Zina Garrison,
former tennis pro

"I'm sure I'll get where I want to go. My parents taught us to believe in ourselves, to have confidence. I can't remember a time I didn't feel good about myself."

Venus Williams

"I don't like putting my name and 'losing' in the same sentence. 'Winning' and 'Venus' sounds great."

Venus Williams

"Sometimes it's good to lose so you can learn. You learn more from when you lose than when you win."

Venus Williams

"Other people say they're confident, but they're really not. We [my sister Venus and I] say it and we mean it. We know how to get what we want."

Serena Williams

ON MAINTAINING A BALANCE:

"Education is more important than tennis right now. Whatever I put in my head will stay there forever, but that's not necessarily true of tennis."

Venus Williams, when she turned pro at age 14

"Richard has done what he thought best for his girls. He gets an A high plus for being the type of parent he is. He's got educated, well-mannered kids who have their priorities in line."

Rick Macci, tennis coach

"There are so many things that I want to do that are more creative [than playing tennis]."

Venus Williams

Strong family support has always been at the heart of Venus's career, providing her with the financial, emotional, and spiritual tools she needs to succeed.

On Her Ability:

"All kids are competitive, but her competitiveness is a couple of levels deeper. She'll run over broken glass to hit a ball."

Rick Macci, tennis coach

"I don't know anyone who's done what Venus did. She should go right to the Hall of Fame. She's going to be there anyway, so why waste time?"

Richard Williams

"I've said it before and I'll say it again, she's got the game and the physique."

Steffi Graf,
former tennis champion

"The key to beating Venus is to return her serves deep so she doesn't blast the next shot for a winner."

Lindsey Davenport,
tennis champion

Dubbed the "ghetto Cinderella" by her father, Venus savored her Wimbledon victory in 2001, top, and finally realized her dream of becoming number 1 the following year.

27

ON HER IMPACT ON THE SPORT:

"I think she's the best athlete the women's game has seen so far. Now it's a matter of how she puts it all together."

    Andre Agassi, tennis champion,
    on Venus at age 17

"Venus is a godsend. She's calling attention to the game, and the game needs that now. She's the Tiger Woods of tennis."

    Bud Collins,
    NBC tennis commentator

"I think with this moment in the first year in Arthur Ashe Stadium, it all represents everyone being together, everyone having a chance to play."

    Venus Williams,
    during the 1997 U.S. Open

Phenomenal strength, agility, and drive have earned Venus accolades from commentator Bud Collins, bottom, and tennis champs such as Andre Agassi, top.

"Tennis has always been a rich man or woman's sport, but now Venus and Serena can change tennis, just like Tiger Woods has done in golf. They've shown that no matter what the color of your skin or how rich you are, you can become a success."

Chris Evert,
former tennis champion

"I admire the way they're [Venus and Serena] unafraid of tennis's virtually all-white press, tennis's virtually all-white locker room, and virtually all-white tennis. They say what they want, say it well and hate to lose . . . the truth is, the Williams family is the best thing to happen to women's tennis since the scrunchee."

Rick Reilly,
Sports Illustrated *writer*

Although ranked number 2 in the world behind Serena, Venus started 2003 in style, keeping the heat on her little sister by going 10–1 in her first 11 tournaments.

OVATIONS